First published in the UK in 2001 by Circle Books

©Circle Books, Dive International Publishing
Aaron House, 6 Bardolph Road
Richmond
Surrey TW9 2LH
Phone: 020 8332 2709
e-mail: email@dive.uk.com

©Donald Tipton
Columbus
Georgia 31907
USA

Editor
Graeme Gourlay

Art Editor
Alison Moffat

Production
Alistair Cook

Printing
Midas
271 King Street
London W6 9LZ
Phone: 020 8741 8011

ISBN 0-9538919-0-9

...and the spirit of God moved upon the face of the waters. And God said 'Let there be light' and there was light. (*Genesis*, chapter 1:2–3)

Upon the face of the waters
by Donald Tipton

Circle Books
London

To my wife Angelyn,

my best friend and only love.

You have borne the burden of

my endeavours

with joy and grace.

**P**hotography is an elusive art form: at times it is impossible to pin down what is a lucky snapshot or what is the work of considered genius; what is a substantial truth and what is a mechanically-captured moment in time. Is the photographer an artist, or a mere recorder of reality? As is often the truth, a body of work is what separates the real artist from the hack, the creative voice distinct from the repetitive babble of the ordinary. And when you look at this collection of Donald Tipton's images you instantly see the connections, the themes, the ideas driving his work.

This is a celebration of the wonder of our seas and the creatures which live in them, a personal testament to the beauty the author has found with his cameras both above and below the sea's surface.

This book is an extended essay on light, an exploration of spatial relationships, a mediation on the diversity of life. It is serious and yet fun. A warning, and a call to arms. Clearly Donald is a gifted photographer, and this is an important work.

Graeme Gourlay

the sections

The gift of seeing is a marvellous thing. It allows us to see into other worlds and to understand. If you imagine that seeing can be like listening to music, then you can realise how it touches the heart. Use the wonderful gift of seeing with the heart as you look upon the face of the waters.

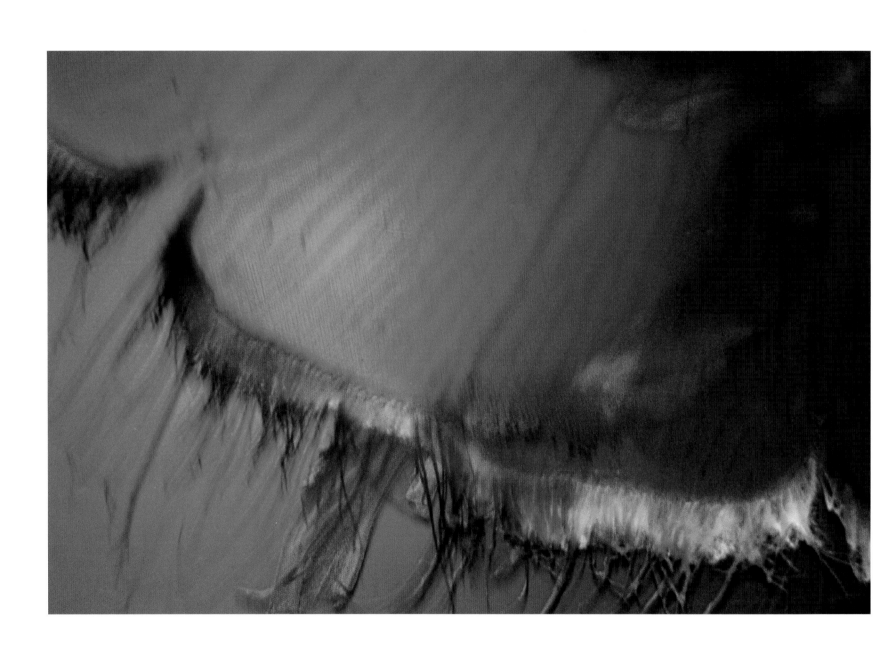

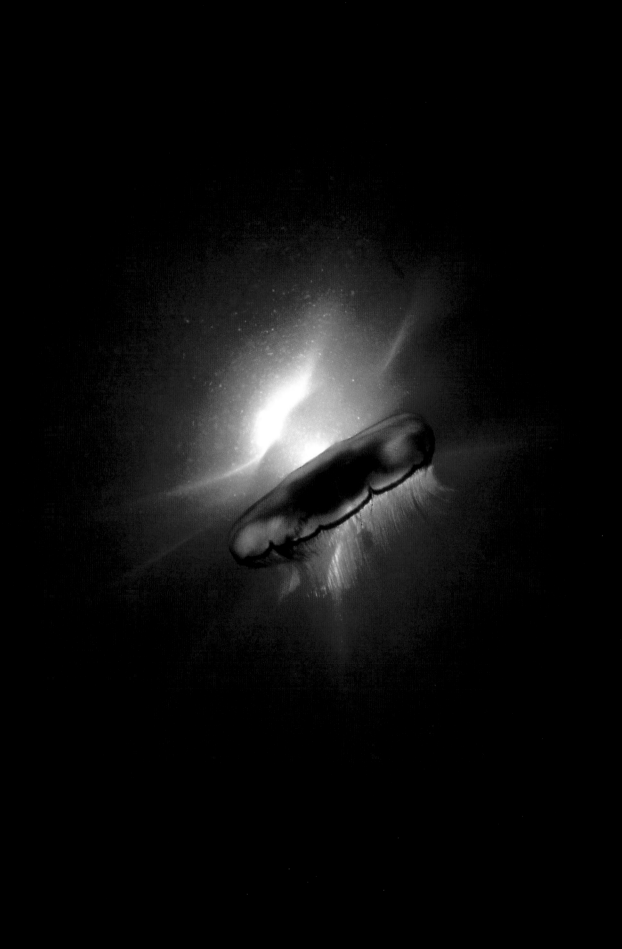

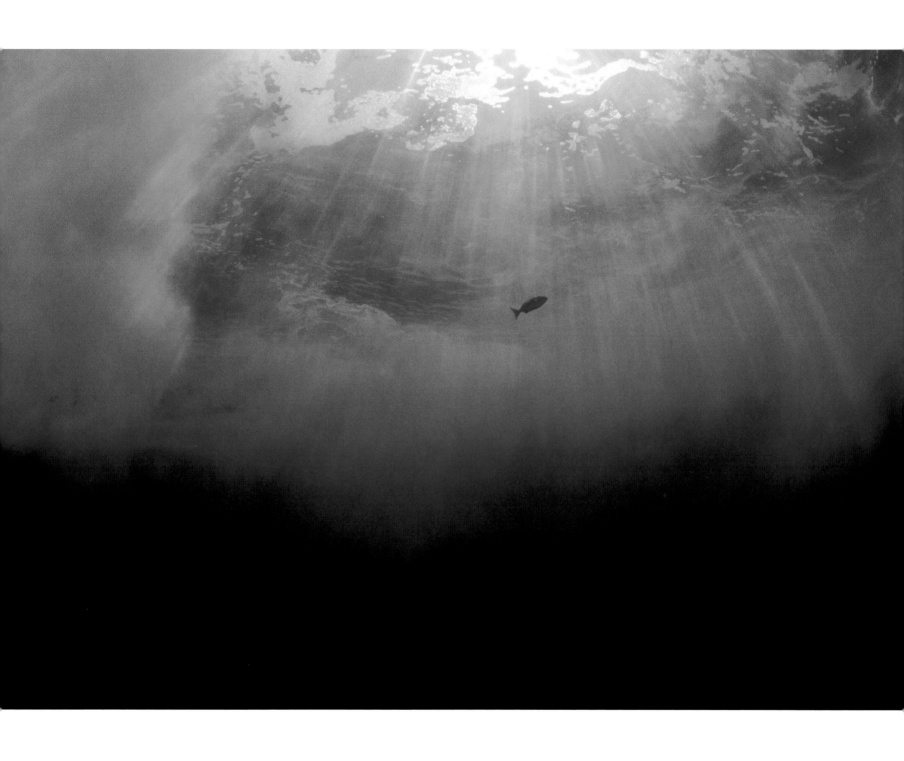

The light of understanding falls upon us all, regardless of genus and species. This light of self-awareness exists, in spite of our preconceptions of intelligence. Understanding, self-awareness and wisdom are all a part of our next step into the light of recognition.

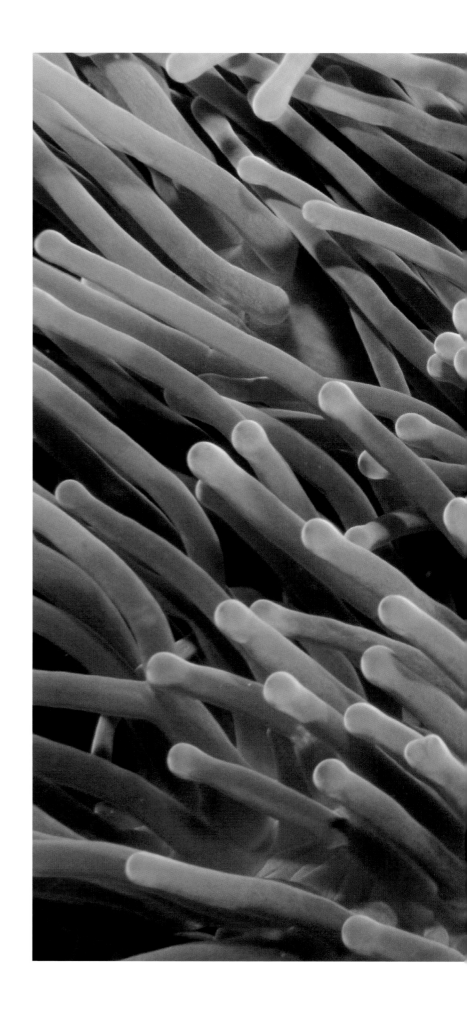

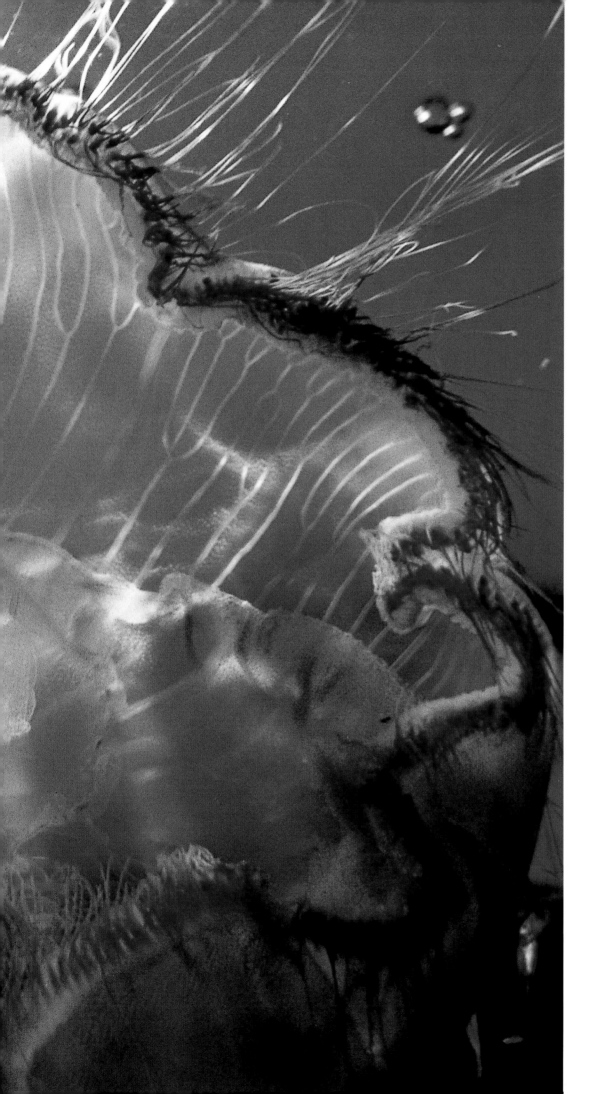

f love is the ultimate expression of truth in the universe, then a mother's love is absolute truth. As with all sentient life forms, the nurturing process is far more than the perpetuation of the species. The long, laborious periods of instruction that enable the child to survive and thrive in a hostile world are the investments of a mother's love. The gentle stroke of fin or arm comfort the child and soothe with a mother's touch.

ince the beginning of recorded history, people have been fascinated by the idea of interspecies communion. And when this communion takes place in the sea, that fascination is even more intense. We are now beginning to understand the true depth of our bond with the sea and its inhabitants. As we look closer into the sea we begin to understand the intelligence of the creatures looking back at us.

big sea

We often fail to understand how things work together as a whole, or fail to see the big picture. Because of this myopic vision, we tend to be aware of only those things that directly affect us. This, I feel, is the principal reason for us having done such harm to the ocean environment. We have failed to understand our oceans, failed to realise their importance and failed to see their connections to the rest of life on this planet. We must urgently begin to look at the BIG SEA.

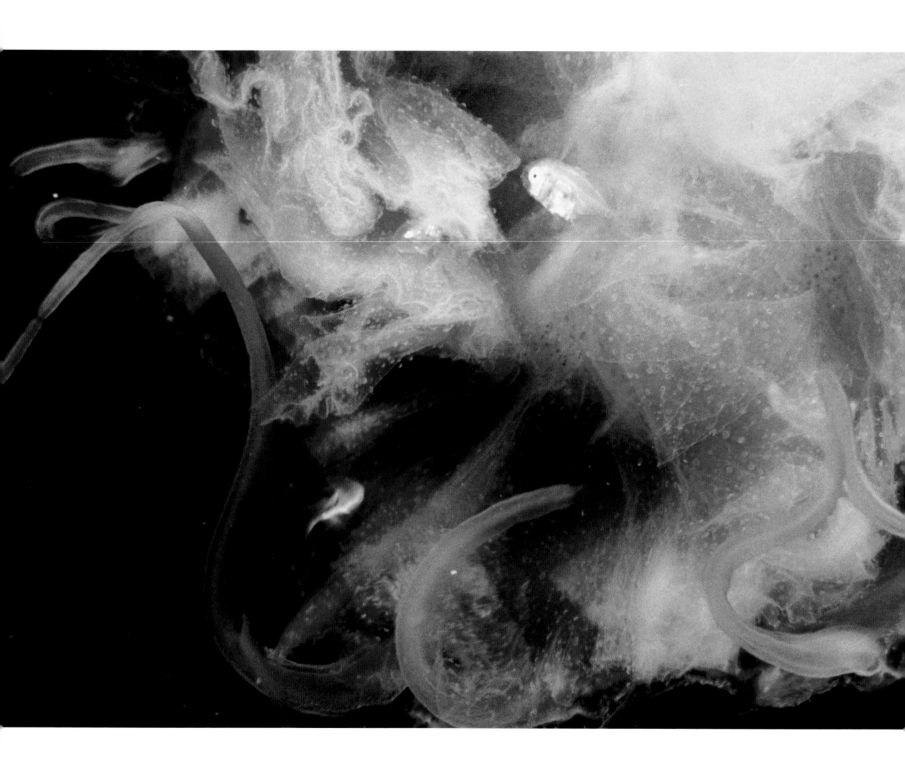

cantabile

The song of the sea is as old as the sea itself. From the beginning, the ocean and all the life in it has sung to the glory of God. Seabirds, like a woodwind section rise high above the booming bass of waves crashing against the shore. Below the surface the intricate counterpoint of whale song plays in absolute harmony with the vast orchestra of the water planet. The pizzicato of dolphin clicks accentuates the pelagic string section of deep ocean currents. Listen.

Shout for joy to the Lord, all the earth,
burst into jubilant song with music;
make music to the Lord with the harp,
with the harp and the sound of singing,
with trumpets and the blast of the ram's horn –
shout for joy before the Lord, the King.

Let the sea resound, and everything in it,
the world, and all who live in it.
Let the rivers clap their hands,
let the mountains sing together for joy;

Let them sing before the Lord,
for He comes to judge the earth.

Psalm 98: 4–9

▲ STORM FRONT ON THE BAHAMA BANK. Sometimes squalls can come out of nowhere, as this one did. By the time I noticed that it was getting dark, it was on me – a wonder of greys and greens. **Nikon 8008, Nikon 28mm lens, Fujichrome Provia 100.**

▼ BOTTLENOSE DOLPHIN, *Tursiops truncatus,* Gulf of Mexico. It is marvellous the way a bottlenose dolphin will look at you. This is the sort of eye contact that seems to penetrate your very being. **Nikon F4S, Aquatica housing, Nikon 18mm lens, Fujichrome Provia 100 film.**

▲ GIANT MANTA RAY *Manta birostris*, Socorro Islands, Mexico. Sometimes when something profound is occurring it doesn't seem real. That is the way I felt with the mantas. **Nikon F4S, Aquatica housing, Nikon 16mm lens, Kodak TMax 100, Ilford Multigrade paper.**

▼ ATLANTIC SPOTTED DOLPHINS, *Stenella frontalis*, Bahama Bank. Nature is art, and it is up to the image maker to see what is already there. **Nikon F4S, Aquatica housing, Nikon 18mm lens, Fujichrome Provia 100.**

▲ BOTTLENOSE DOLPHIN, *Tursiops truncatus,* Gulf of Mexico page 3. in the early evening, if the wind is not blowing too much, the sea can take on a creamy texture, like black milk. On this evening, there didn't seem to be a puff of wind as this young dolphin surfaced. **Nikon 8008, Nikon 28mm lens, Fujichrome Provia 100.**

▼ SILKY SHARK WITH PILOTFISH, *Carcharhinus falciformis,* Socorro Islands, Mexico, page 5. It is amazing how everything in the sea works together for survival and at the same time competes. **Nikon F4S, Aquatica housing, Nikon 16mm lens, Ikelite 200 strobes, Fujichrome Provia 100.**

▲ CALIFORNIA SEA LION, *Zalophus californianus,* Anacappa Island, California, page 6. The sea lion was heading straight for the surface at phenomenal speed. This is the marine creature for me – the essence of form and beauty. **Nikon F4S, Aquatica housing, Nikon 18mm lens, Kodak TMAX 400 film, Ilford Multigrade paper.**

▾ A BOTTLENOSE DOLPHIN, *Tursiops truncatus,* page 9. In the background is the shallow water and barrier island off the Florida Panhandle. The dolphin simply swam over and had a look at me, and left as quickly as he came. **Nikon FE2, Fujichrome Sensia 100.**

▲ SUMMER STORM, Gulf of Mexico, page 10. This storm reminded me of a painting, as it moved towards the shore. I became enthralled with its beauty, and almost forgot to cover my camera when it started raining. **Nikon F4S, 28mm lens, Fujichrome Provia 100.**

▾ WATER SPOUT, Bimini, Bahamas, page 11. This water spout appeared when we were about half a mile away and I took this image. To me it was a comfortable distance, close enough for the picture, far enough for safety. **Nikon F4S, Nikon 300mm lens, Fujichrome Provia 100.**

▲ MOON JELLYFISH, *Aurelia aurita,* Gulf of Mexico, page 12. There are some animals you are not meant to get too close to! The pink tentacles against the greenish water is what makes this picture for me – and it was worth getting that close. **Nikon FE2, Ikelite housing, 55mm macro lens, Ikelite 150 strobe, Fujichrome Provia 100.**

▾ MOON JELLYFISH BY SUNLIGHT, page 13. Sometimes a potentially wonderful photograph is not so obvious. The opportunity for this image came about after I had followed the progress of this little jellyfish through the ocean. **Nikon F4S, Nikon 16mm lens, Fujichrome Provia 100.**

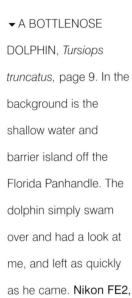

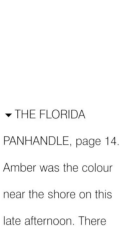

▲ FREEPORT, BAHAMAS, page 14. The cool blue of the early light of day. **Nikon F4S, 28mm lens, Fujichrome Provia 100. No filter.**

▼ THE FLORIDA PANHANDLE, page 14. Amber was the colour near the shore on this late afternoon. There had been only the slightest breeze over the Gulf of Mexico that day. **Nikon 8008, 28mm lens, Fujichrome Provia 100. No filter.**

▲ CALIFORNIA SEA LION, *Zalophus californianus,* Anacappa Island, California, page 15. The joy of flying. **Nikon F4S, Aquatica housing, 18mm lens, Kodak TMAX, Illford Multigrade paper.**

▼ TWO ATLANTIC SPOTTED DOLPHINS, *Stenella frontalis*, Bahamas, page 16. These dolphins and I had a wonderful game of racing to the surface. Of course, the dolphins always won. That was okay, because I was able to get the shot. **Nikon F4S, 16mm lens, Kodak TMAX 100.**

▲ SOUTHERN STINGRAY, *Dasyatis americana,* Bimini, Bahamas, page 17. I used a Dräger Dolphin Rebreather to get close to this stingray. **Nikon F4S, Aquatica, 16mm lens, Kodak TMAX 100.**

▼ LION'S MANE, *Cyanea capillata*, Gulf of Mexico. page 18. A particularly difficult animal to photograph since its tentacles are transparent and carry a strong sting. The idea is to get close enough and hope that the current doesn't shift. **Nikon F4S, Aquatica housing, Nikon 18mm lens, Ilelite 200 strobe, Fujichrome Provia 100.**

▲ JUVENILE ATLANTIC SPOTTED DOLPHIN, *Stenella frontalis*, Bahama Bank, page 19. This young dolphin seemed to be mesmerised in the beautiful sunlight, just as I was. Beams of sunlight underwater can be amazing. **Nikon F4S, Aquatica, 16mm lens, Fujichrome Provia 100.**

▼ TWO LAUGHING GULLS, Panama City Beach, Florida, page 21. It is amazing that sea birds are so well adapted for the air, ocean, and the land. These birds seem to soar so effortlessly into the late afternoon sun. **Nikon 8008, Nikon 300mm lens, Fujichrome Sensia 100.**

▲ PACIFIC ATOLL FROM 35,000 FEET, page 22. At the top of the image, space, air and sea seem to meet as one. The next time you fly, watch for this wonder of Earth's beauty. **Nikon 8008, Nikon 28mm lens. Fujichrome Provia 100.**

▼ BANDOS ISLAND, MALDIVES, Indian Ocean, page 23. I am always fascinated by the change from sea to sky. **Nikon F4S, Nikon 28 lens, Fujichrome Provia 100.**

▲ BOTTLENOSE DOLPHIN, *Tursiops truncatus*, Cayman Brac, page 24. Spot was a wild dolphin who for about a year was happy to play with divers. **Nikon F4S, Aquatica housing, Nikon 16mm lens, Kodak TMax 100, Ilford Multigrade paper.**

▼ UNDER A BIG WAVE, Archipelago de Revillagigedo, Mexico, page 25. I was hoping to find and photograph manta rays in this dramatic setting. **Nikon F4S, Aquatica housing, Nikon 16mm lens, Ikelite strobes, Fujichrome Provia 100.**

▼ BOTTLENOSE DOLPHIN AND HERRING GULL *Tursiops truncatus, Larus argentatus,* northern Gulf of Mexico, page 26. The marvellous thing is that when I shot this, I had no idea the bird was there: I didn't see it until I was editing my images. **Nikon 8008, Sigma 14mm lens, Fujichrome Sensia 100.**

▲ BABY HUMPBACK WHALE, *Megaptera novaeangliae,* Silver Bank, Dominican Republic, page 28. One of the breaks for photographers is that baby humpback whales tend to be very curious. This baby was 2ft from my camera. **Nikon F4S, Aquatica housing, Nikon 18mm lens, Kodak TMAX 100, Ilford Multigrade paper.**

▼ BABY HUMPBACK WHALE, *Megaptera novaeangliae,* Silver Bank, Dominican Republic, page 30. Large numbers of humpbacks gather around Silver Bank, an isolated reef in the Caribbean. **Nikon F4S, Aquatica housing, Nikon 18mm lens, Kodak TMAX 100, Ilford Multigrade paper.**

▲ BABY HUMPBACK WHALE, *Megaptera novaeangliae,* Silver Bank, Dominican Republic, page 31. This curious young whale and I considered one another for a moment or two, but all too soon mother whale said it was time to go. **Nikon F4S, Aquatica housing, Nikon 18mm lens, Kodak TMAX 100, Ilford Multigrade paper.**

▼ CALIFORNIAN SEA LION, *Zalophus californianus,* Anacappa Island, California, page 32. The light and the sandy sea floor made a great background to work with. The sea lion was great to work with too! **Nikon F4S, Aquatica housing, Nikon 18mm lens, Kodak TMAX 100, Ilford Multigrade paper.**

▲ JUVENILE BOT-TLENOSE DOLPHIN, *Tursiops truncatus,* Gulf of Mexico, page 33. I have known this male dolphin for several years. This image was shot in the summer of 1994 when he was about four or five years old. Nikon FE2, Ikelite housing, 17mm lens, Fujichrome Sensia 100.

▾ CALIFORNIA SEA LION, *Zalophus californianus,* Channel Islands, California, page 34. The sub-adult sea lions are the most playful and curious, making them ideal photographic models. Nikon F4S, Aquatica housing, Nikon 18mm lens, Ikelite 200 strobe, Fujichrome Provia 100.

▲ HAWAIIAN MONK SEAL, *Monachus schauinslandi,* Midway Island, Pacific, page 35. At the end of my dive I noticed this guy diving a small school of fish, but he didn't seem to be catching anything. He did, however, seem to be having a lot of fun. Nikon F4S, Aquatica housing, Nikon 16mm lens, Fujichrome Provia 100.

▾ ATLANTIC SPOTTED DOLPHINS, *Stenella frontalis,* Bahama Bank, page 35. Play seems to be the order of business with most species of dolphin. This is especially the case with the spotted dolphins of the Bahama Bank. Nikon 8008, Aquatica housing, Sigma 14mm lens, Fujichrome Sensia 100.

▲ GALÁPAGOS SHARK, *Carcharhinus galapagensis,* Midway Island, Pacific, page 36. The sharks here have rarely seen divers and are very curious. These are magnificently beautiful and move like poetry. Nikon F4S, Aquatica housing, Sigma 14mm lens, Ikelite 200 strobes, Kodak TMAX 100, Ilford Multigrade paper.

▾ SOUTHERN STINGRAY, *Dasyatis americana,* Grand Cayman, page 37. The stingray is one of the strangest looking creatures in the sea but one of the most beautiful. We were free-diving at on a shallow sand flat when I met this one. Nikon F4S, Nikon16mm lens, Kodak T-Max 100, Ilford Multigrade paper.

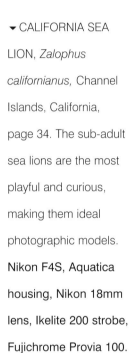

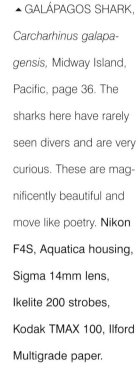

▲ CALIFORNIA SEA LION, *Zalophus californianus,* Channel Islands, California, page 38. After seeing this young sea lion drag its belly in the sand, I wondered if it might be fun. Well, I gave it a go and discovered that it was. **Nikon F4S, Aquatica housing, Nikon 18mm lens, Ikelite strobe, Kodak TMAX 100, Ilford Multigrade paper.**

▼ SUB-ADULT CALIFORNIA SEA LION, *Zalophus californianus,* Monterey Bay, California, page 39. The sea lion, like other pinnipeds, spends part of its life on land. This young female was resting in the sun after a morning swim. **Nikon 8008, Nikon 300mm lens, Kodak TMAX 100.**

▲ BROWN PELICAN, *Pelecanus occidentalis,* Florida, page 40. The pelican was looking for its next meal and sitting quite comfortably on the jetty at Saint Andrew's Bay, Panama City. These birds are so much fun to watch – when they land in the water it is a controlled crash. **Nikon F4S, Nikon 300mm lens, Fujichrome Provia 100.**

▼ NORTHERN ELEPHANT SEAL, *Mirounga angustirostris,* Ano Nuevo, California, page 41. This big male was clearly saying that I had better not come any closer. I was told by the rangers to stay 100ft away, which I did. I was glad that I had a long lens. **Nikon F4S, Nikon 400mm lens, Fujichrome Provia 100.**

▲ FLORIDA MANATEE, *Trichechus manatus,* Crystal River, Florida, page 42. The Florida manatee spends its winters in the warm-water springs along the coast – a great place to photograph these gentle herbivores, since the springs are usually very clear. **Nikon 8008, Aquatica housing, Sigma 14mm lens, Fujichrome Provia 100.**

▼ BOTTLENOSE DOLPHIN, *Tursiops truncatus,* Gulf of Mexico, page 43. The dolphin was spy-hopping beside the boat, with the setting sun in the background. After several jumps it occurred to me that I was missing a great shot. **Nikon 8008, Sigma 14mm lens, Kodak TMAX 100, Ilford Multigrade paper.**

▲ CLOWN ANEMONE FISH, *Amphiprion nigripes,* Maldives, page 44 and 45. This clownfish and I had a grand old time looking at one another. I think the fish knew that I wasn't particularly fond of macro photography, so he gave me a bit of a show. **Nikon F4S, Nikon 60mm macro lens, two Ikelite 200 strobes, Fujichrome Provia 100.**

▼ TWO ATLANTIC SPOTTED DOLPHINS, *Stenella frontalis,* Bahama Bank, page 46. I swam with these two for quite some time, in slow circles, spiralling up. As we swam, the circle became smaller and the eye contact more intense. **Nikon F4S, Aquatica housing, Kodak TMAX 100, Ilford Multigrade paper.**

▲ TWO BOTTLENOSE DOLPHINS, *Tursiops truncatus,* Gulf of Mexico, page 47. These two dolphins were having a bit of a game with me, in which they would swim up from behind me as though to say 'Boo'! **Nikon F4S, Aquatica housing, Nikon 16mm lens, Kodak TMAX 100, Ilford Multigrade paper.**

▼ BOTTLENOSE DOLPHIN, *Tursiops truncatus*, Gulf of Mexico, page 48. I was waiting on the bottom for this dolphin to swim by, but instead it swam over me. I was lucky to catch it in front of the sun. **Nikon 8008, Sigma 14mm lens, Kodak TMAX 100, Ilford Multigrade paper.**

▲ BOTTLENOSE DOLPHIN, *Tursiops truncatus,* Gulf of Mexico, page 49. The dolphin and I were together just for a moment as we swam together into the light. **Nikon 8008, Sigma 14mm lens, Kodak TMAX 100, Ilford Multigrade paper.**

▼ FEATHER BLENNY, *Hypsoblennius bentzi,* Gulf of Mexico, page 50. This little guy is so small, he lives in this barnacle. Yet he is very big on eye contact. **Nikon FE2, Ikelite housing, Nikon 55mm macro lens, Ikelite 150 strobe, Fujichrome Sensia 100.**

▼ CALIFORNIA SHORE, just north of Los Angeles, page 51. We were riding along the coast just as the magic of the sunset started to happen. It was a mad dash to try to find a beach entrance and get to the shore. **Nikon F4S, Nikon 28mm lens, Fujichrome Provia 100.**

▲ MOON JELLYFISH, *Aurelia aurita,* Gulf of Mexico, page 52 and 53. This jellyfish was only about a foot across, and I was very close to it. Luckily, I had a camera housing between us. **Nikon FE2, Ikelite housing, Nikkor 55 macro lens, Kodak EPP 100 film.**

▼ BABY HUMPBACK WHALE, *Megaptera novaeangliae,* Silver Bank, Dominican Republic, page 54 and 55. This baby whale was born into a sea of sound. All the male humpback whales sing while they are on the mating grounds of the Silver Bank. **Nikon F4S, Aquatica housing, Nikon 18mm lens, Fujichrome Provia 100.**

▲ MOTHER AND BABY BOTTLENOSE DOLPHINS, *Tursiops truncatus,* Gulf of Mexico, page 56. The mother is giving the baby dolphin a little help with swimming. **Nikon FE2, Ikelite housing, 17mm lens, Kodak TMax 400, Ilford Multigrade paper.**

▼ TWO HUMANS, *Homo sapiens*, Gulf of Mexico, near Panama City Beach, Florida, page 58. The adult is Natalie Richard, wife of Denis Richard, founder of Water Planet. The child is Aisia, Denis's daughter. **Nikon F4S, Aquatica housing, Nikon 16mm lens, Fujichrome Sensia 100.**

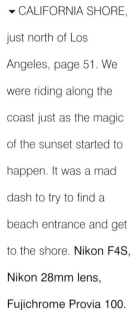

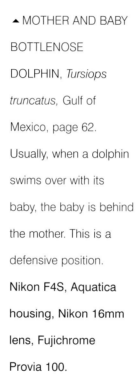

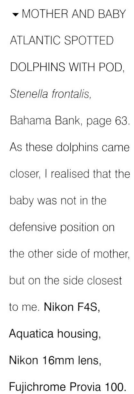

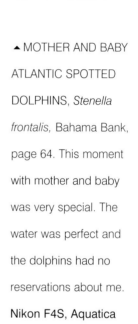

▲ TWO HUMANS, *Homo sapiens,* Gulf of Mexico, near Panama City Beach, Florida, page 59. There are lots of ways to learn free-diving and I suppose that this is just as good as any of them. **Nikon F4S, Aquatica housing, Nikon 16mm lens, Kodak TMAX 100, Ilford Multigrade paper.**

▼ MOTHER AND BABY HUMPBACK WHALE, *Megaptera novaeangliae,* Silver Bank, Dominican Republic, page 60. The baby was very active, swimming about, while mother was calmly swimming below. **Nikon F4S, Aquatica housing, Nikon 16mm lens, Fujichrome Provia 100.**

▲ MOTHER AND BABY BOTTLENOSE DOLPHIN, *Tursiops truncatus,* Gulf of Mexico, page 62. Usually, when a dolphin swims over with its baby, the baby is behind the mother. This is a defensive position. **Nikon F4S, Aquatica housing, Nikon 16mm lens, Fujichrome Provia 100.**

▼ MOTHER AND BABY ATLANTIC SPOTTED DOLPHINS WITH POD, *Stenella frontalis,* Bahama Bank, page 63. As these dolphins came closer, I realised that the baby was not in the defensive position on the other side of mother, but on the side closest to me. **Nikon F4S, Aquatica housing, Nikon 16mm lens, Fujichrome Provia 100.**

▲ MOTHER AND BABY ATLANTIC SPOTTED DOLPHINS, *Stenella frontalis,* Bahama Bank, page 64. This moment with mother and baby was very special. The water was perfect and the dolphins had no reservations about me. **Nikon F4S, Aquatica housing, Nikon 16mm lens, Kodak TMAX 100, Ilford Multigrade paper.**

▼ MOTHER AND BABY ATLANTIC SPOTTED DOLPHINS, *Stenella frontalis,* Bahama Bank, page 65. Light, and the way it behaves underwater, fascinates me. This image is about the light and the baby's response to it. **Nikon F4S, Aquatica housing, Nikon 18mm lens, Kodak TMAX 100, Ilford Multigrade paper.**

▲ YOUNG ATLANTIC SPOTTED DOLPHIN, *Stenella frontalis,* Bahama Bank, page 66 and 67. Dolphins respond to the sea. If the water is rough, they do a lot of jumping. If the water is flat calm like this, they seem to swim quietly. **Nikon F4S, Aquatica housing, Nikon 16mm lens, Kodak TMAX 100. Ilford Multigrade paper.**

▼ MOTHER AND BABY ATLANTIC SPOTTED DOLPHINS, *Stenella frontalis,* Bahama Bank, page 68. When the dolphins swam over I had to decide whether to shoot surface stuff, or whether to get in the water. Given the rarity of surface images of dolphins in this book, you can guess what I normally decide. **Nikon F4S, Nikon 28mm lens, Fujichrome Provia 100.**

▲ MOTHER AND BABY BOTTLENOSE DOLPHINS, *Tursiops truncatus,* Gulf of Mexico, page 69. Mother and baby marine mammals spend a great deal of time touching. This is a very defensive position for this baby. **Nikon F4S, Aquatica housing, Nikon 18mm lens, Kodak TMAX 100, Ilford Multigrade paper.**

▼ MOTHER AND BABY MANATEES, *Trichechus manatus*, Crystal River, Florida, page 70. I was alone in this spring except for these two manatees. I fired off a few frames, then my camera jammed. **Nikon 8008, Aquatica housing, Sigma 14mm lens, Fujichrome Provia 100.**

▲ TWO FLORIDA MANATEES, *Trichechus manatus,* Crystal River, Florida, page 71. These two manatees seemed to be saying hello to each other. It reminds me of a mother kissing her daughter goodbye, on the forehead. **Nikon F4S, Aquatica housing, 16mm lens, Fujichrome Provia 100.**

▼ BABY FLORIDA MANATEE, *Trichechus manatus,* Crystal River, Florida, page 72. Young manatees have all sorts of games they like to play, such as rolling in mud. I particularly like this one as it reminds me of myself at that age. **Nikon F4S, Aquatica housing, 16mm lens, Fujichrome Provia 100.**

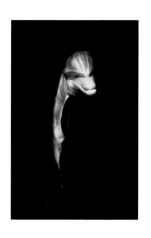

▲ MANATEES, *Trichechus manatus,* Crystal River, Florida, page 74. Is this wildlife voyeurism or is it a study in animal behaviour? **Nikon F4S, Aquatica housing, Nikon 16mm lens, Kodak TMAX 100, Ilford Multigrade paper.**

▼ MOTHER AND BABY MANATEES, *Trichechus manatus,* Crystal River, Florida, page 75. The baby had been nursing when the mother abruptly decided to swim my way. As you can see, the baby had not exactly finished with lunch. **Nikon F4S, Aquatica housing, Nikon 16mm lens, Fujichrome Provia 100.**

▲ HUMPBACK WHALE, *Megaptera novaeangliae,* Silver Bank, Dominican Republic, page 76. Young humpback whales frequently travel on their mothers' backs – the touch of the mother reassures the baby. **Nikon F4S, Aquatica housing, Nikon 18mm lens, Fujichrome Provia 100.**

▼ HUMPBACK WHALES, *Megaptera novaeangliae,* Silver Bank, Dominican Republic, page 77. The seas on the Silver Bank can be quite rough at times. This little baby whale has just slapped its flukes against the torrent of waves above. **Nikon F4S, Aquatica housing, Nikon 18mm lens, Kodak TMAX 100, Ilford Multigrade paper.**

▲ BOTTLENOSE DOLPHIN, *Tursiops truncatus,* Gulf of Mexico, page 78. When a dolphin looks at you, it literally sees right through you. They see with sound – they use ultrasound to read you inside and out. **Nikon FE2, Ikelite housing, 17mm lens, Kodak TMAX 400, Ilford Multigrade paper.**

▲ BOTTLENOSE DOLPHIN AND HUMAN, *Tursiops truncatus, Homo sapiens*, Gulf of Mexico, page 80. This is my friend, Cathy Nessins, from Belgium. She is not only a great diver, but she is a dancer as well. **Nikon F4S, Aquatica housing, Nikon 18mm lens, Kodak TMAX 100, Ilford Multigrade paper.**

▼ BOTTLENOSE DOLPHIN AND HUMAN, *Tursiops truncatus, Homo sapiens,* Gulf of Mexico, page 81. Kim Spencer is a great model, diver and Mom. **Nikon F4S, Aquatica housing, Nikon 18mm lens, Ikelite 150 strobes, Kodak TMAX 100, Ilford Multigrade paper.**

▲ BOTTLENOSE DOLPHIN AND HUMAN CHILD, *Tursiops truncatus* and *Homo sapiens,* Gulf of Mexico, 82 and back cover. This image has had a profound effect on me since it was made. The child is the seven month-old daughter of friends. **Nikon FE2, Ikelite housing, 17mm lens, Kodak EPP 100 film.**

▼ BOTTLENOSE DOLPHIN AND HUMAN CHILD, *Tursiops truncatus* and *Homo sapiens,* Gulf of Mexico, page 83. Throughout this shoot with a wild dolphin the mother of the baby was close at hand in the water – in fact, of 72 exposures there are only four in which she doesn't appear. **Nikon FE2, Ikelite housing, 17mm lens, Kodak EPP 100 film.**

▲ HUMAN BABY AND BOTTLENOSE DOLPHIN, *Homo sapiens, Tursiops truncatus,* Gulf of Mexico, page 84. This image records one of those defining moments. In the innocence of this child, I see humanity's hope. **Nikon FE2, Ikelite housing, 17mm lens, Kodak TMAX 400, Ilford Multigrade paper.**

▼ BOTTLENOSE DOLPHIN AND HUMAN, *Tursiops truncatus, Homo sapiens,* Gulf of Mexico, page 85. The model is April, who worked with the Human Dolphin Institute in Florida for a summer. **Nikon F4S, Aquatica housing, Nikon 18mm lens, Kodak TMAX 100, Ilford Multigrade paper.**

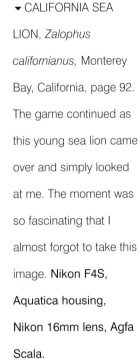

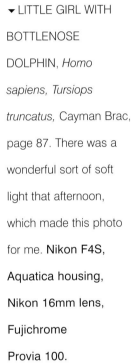

▲ ATLANTIC SPOTTED DOLPHIN AND HUMAN, *Stenella frontalis, Homo sapiens,* Bahama Bank, page 86. The diver, Cedric Atlas, is a dear friend and the son of Michael Atlas, the founder of The Human Dolphin Institute in Florida. **Nikon 8008s, Aquatica housing, Sigma 14mm lens, Fujichrome Provia 100.**

▼ LITTLE GIRL WITH BOTTLENOSE DOLPHIN, *Homo sapiens, Tursiops truncatus,* Cayman Brac, page 87. There was a wonderful sort of soft light that afternoon, which made this photo for me. **Nikon F4S, Aquatica housing, Nikon 16mm lens, Fujichrome Provia 100.**

▲ ATLANTIC SPOTTED DOLPHIN AND HUMAN, *Stenella frontalis, Homo sapiens,* Bimini, Bahamas, page 88. Capt Stewart Turner is a great free-diver. Dolphins seem to appreciate this. **Nikon F4S, Aquatica housing, Nikon 18mm lens, Kodak TMAX 100, Ilford Multigrade paper.**

▼ BOTTLENOSE DOLPHIN AND HUMAN, *Tursiops truncatus, Homo sapiens,* Gulf of Mexico, page 89. I often use rebreathers, as lots of creatures don't like air bubbles. **Nikon F4S, Aquatica housing, Nikon 18mm lens, Ikelite 200 strobes, Kodak TMAX 100, Ilford Multigrade paper.**

▲ BOTTLENOSE DOLPHIN AND MY DAUGHTER KATHERINE *Tursiops truncatus*, Gulf of Mexico, page 90. Of course I'm biased but my daughter does seem to have a way with dolphins. This doesn't seem unreasonable, since I have been using her for 'bait' since she was two years old. **Nikon F4S, Aquatica housing, Nikon 18mm lens, Fujichrome Provia 100.**

▼ CALIFORNIA SEA LION, *Zalophus californianus,* Monterey Bay, California, page 92. The game continued as this young sea lion came over and simply looked at me. The moment was so fascinating that I almost forgot to take this image. **Nikon F4S, Aquatica housing, Nikon 16mm lens, Agfa Scala.**

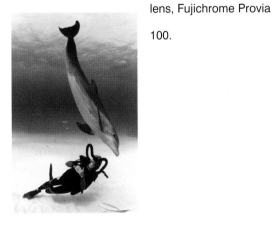

▼ CALIFORNIA SEA LION, *Zalophus californianus,* Monterey Bay, page 93. We were diving in a shallow bay that was full of sea lions. When I found a good position on the bottom, they started to dive-bomb my camera. Nikon F4S, Aquatica housing, Nikon 16mm lens, Agfa Scala.

▲ BOTTLENOSE DOLPHIN, *Tursiops truncatus,* Gulf of Mexico, page 94. Light in the sea is a marvellous thing. The dolphin came over to me to have a look and share the light. **Nikon F4S, Aquatica housing,** Nikon 18mm lens, Fujichrome Provia 100.

▼ ATLANTIC SPOTTED DOLPHIN, *Stenella frontalis,* Bahama Bank, page 95. The dolphins of the Bahama Bank love to swim over and make eye contact. This one had a gaze that seemed to go right through me. Nikon F4S, Aquatica housing, Nikon 16mm lens, Fujichrome Provia 100.

▲ NAPOLEON WRASSE *Cheilinus undulatus,* Maldives, page 96. I was at the end of my dive when this gentle giant swam by. **Nikon F4S, Aquatica housing,** Nikon 18mm lens, Ikelite 200 strobes, Fujichrome Provia 100.

▼ GREEN TURTLE *Chelonia mydas,* Midway Atoll, page 98. This turtle seemed to make a home of this shallow wreck. I visited the site several times and the turtle was always nearby. Nikon F4S, Aquatica housing, Nikon 16mm lens, Ikelite strobes, Fujichrome Provia 100.

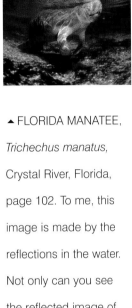

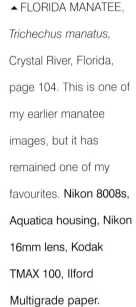

▲ USS MACAW, Midway Atoll, Pacific, page 100. The Macaw was a US Navy minesweeper that went down in a storm in 1943. **Nikon F4S, Aquatica housing, Nikon 16mm lens, Kodak TMAX 100, Ilford Multigrade paper.**

▼ GREEN TURTLE, *Chelonia mydas*, Midway Atoll, Pacific, page 101. This image was the last frame on the roll. I really wanted to work more, but I was grateful for what I was given. **Nikon F4S, 18mm lens, Ikelite 200 strobes, Fujichrome Provia 100.**

▲ FLORIDA MANATEE, *Trichechus manatus,* Crystal River, Florida, page 102. To me, this image is made by the reflections in the water. Not only can you see the reflected image of the manatee, but the trees surrounding the spring as well. **Nikon F4S, Aquatica housing, Nikon 16mm lens, Ikelite 150 strobe, Fujichrome Provia 100.**

▼ YOUNG MANATEE, *Trichechus manatus,* Crystal River, Florida, page 103. It was a very quiet day. There were just a few manatees and no other people around, which is exactly the way I like it. **Nikon F4S, Aquatica housing, Nikon 16mm lens, Kodak TMAX 100, Ilford Multigrade paper.**

▲ FLORIDA MANATEE, *Trichechus manatus,* Crystal River, Florida, page 104. This is one of my earlier manatee images, but it has remained one of my favourites. **Nikon 8008s, Aquatica housing, Nikon 16mm lens, Kodak TMAX 100, Ilford Multigrade paper.**

▼ FLORIDA MANATEE, *Trichechus manatus,* Crystal River, Florida, page 105. I was pleased that this image helped to illustrate the two worlds of marine mammals. **Nikon F4S, Aquatica housing, Nikon 16mm lens, Kodak TMAX 100, Ilford Multigrade paper.**

▲ CALIFORNIA SEA
LIONS, *Zalophus
californianus,* Anacappa
Island, California, page
106. This group of sub-
adult males wanted to
play a game of tag. I
was 'it'. **Nikon F4S,
16mm lens, Ikelite 200
strobes, Kodak
TMAX 100, Ilford
Multigrade paper.**

▼ ATLANTIC SPOTTED
DOLPHINS, *Stenella
frontalis,* Bahama Bank,
page 107. These
dolphins seemed as if
they were posing for this
picture. Actually, they
were just moving their
heads around to get a
better sonar picture of
me. **Nikon F4S,16mm
lens, Ikelite 200 strobes,
Kodak TMAX 100, Ilford
Multigrade paper.**

▲ CALIFORNIA SEA
LIONS, *Zalophus
californianus,* Anacappa
Island, California, page
108. This young sea lion
seemed to want to play
more than the others.
He would make tight
circles around me.
**Nikon F4S, 18mm lens,
Ikelite 200 strobes,
Kodak TMAX 100,
Multigrade paper.**

▼ BOTTLENOSE
DOLPHINS, *Tursiops
truncatus,* Gulf of
Mexico, page 109. This
group of dolphins had
been interacting, but
had decided to move
on. A single dolphin
came closer, to say
goodbye. **Nikon F4S,
16mm lens, Ikelite 200
strobes, Kodak TMAX
100, Ilford Multigrade
paper.**

▲ MOON JELLYFISH
Aurelia aurita, Gulf of
Mexico, page 110. While
an encounter with this
creature could be
potentualy painful, it is
also amazing. **Nikon
FE2, Ikelite housing,
Nikon 55mm lens,
Ikelite 150 strobe,
Kodak EPP 100.**

▼ REEF SCENE WITH
QUEEN ANGELFISH,
Pelancar Reef, Cozumel,
page 111. My wife
doesn't like this image,
but she was in the water
with me when I took it
and for that reason
alone I like it. **Nikon
8008s, Aquatica
housing, Sigma 14mm
lens, Ikelite 150
strobes, Fujichrome
Sensia 100.**

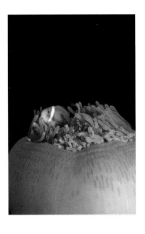

▲ ANEMONEFISH, *Amphiprion nigripes,* Maldives, page112. The anemonefish and the anemone are such a beautiful example of the harmony of symbiosis. **Nikon F4S, Aquatica housing, Nikon 60mm macro, Ikelite strobes, Fujichrome Provia 100.**

▼ BAHAMA BANK, page 113. This hot afternoon on the bank was absolutely wonderful. After playing all morning in the warm water with dolphins, I noticed this little cumulus cloud building on the horizon. **Nikon F4S, 28mm lens, Fujichrome Provia 100.**

▲ BABY HUMPBACK WHALE, *Megaptera novaeangliae,* Silver Bank, Dominican Republic, page 114 and 115. This baby was playing on the surface. It had come up for a breath of air and a slash of its tail. **Nikon F4S, Aquatica housing, Nikon 18mm lens, Fujichrome Provia 100.**

▼ ATLANTIC SPOTTED DOLPHIN, *Stenella frontalis,* Bahama Bank, page 116. I felt as if I were in a ballet, and this dolphin was the star. He seems to be suspended in air, as if God had just placed him there. **Nikon F4S, Aquatica housing, Nikon 18mm lens, Fujichrome Provia 100.**

▲ ATLANTIC SPOTTED DOLPHINS, *Stenella frontalis,* Bahama Bank, page 117. This group of dolphins had just come over to play with us. These agile creatures never seem to get tired of their endless games. If only we could keep up. **Nikon F4S, Aquatica housing, Nikon 18mm lens, Fujichrome Provia 100.**

▲ ATLANTIC SPOTTED DOLPHIN, *Stenella frontalis,* Bahama Bank, page 118. On this late afternoon we were joined by a couple of friendly dolphins. The afternoon sunlight was beautiful, shimmering on the waves and through the water column. **Nikon F4S, Aquatica housing, Nikon 16mm lens, Fujichrome Provia 100.**

▼ ATLANTIC SPOTTED DOLPHIN, *Stenella frontalis,* Bahama Bank, page 119. This juvenile dolphin was as curious about me as I was of him. The flat calm was only broken by his occasional splash as he played nearby. **Nikon F4S, Aquatica housing, Nikon 16mm lens, Fujichrome Provia 100.**

▲ ATLANTIC SPOTTED DOLPHINS, *Stenella frontalis,* Bahama Bank, page 120. This pod of dolphins swam through for a quick visit. They were only here long enough for this parting shot. **Nikon F4S, Aquatica housing, Nikon 16mm lens, Fujichrome Provia 100.**

▼ FLORIDA MANATEE, *Trichechus manatus,* Crystal River, Florida, page 122. In one of the shallow springs of Crystal River, this manatee and I became friends. **Nikon F4S, Aquatica housing, Nikon 16mm lens, Fujichrome Provia 100.**

▲ FLORIDA MANATEE, *Trichechus manatus,* Crystal River, Florida, page 123. This image makes me think about the manatee's plight: he is coming out of the gloomy water and could easily vanish forever. **Nikon F4S, Aquatica housing, Nikon 16mm lens, Fujichrome Provia 100.**

▼ BOTTLENOSE DOLPHIN, *Tursiops truncatus*, Cayman Brac, page 124. Spot, the dolphin, seemed to demand that the divers he encountered make physical contact. **Nikon F4S, Aquatica housing, Nikon 16mm lens, Kodak TMax 100, Ilford Multigrade paper.**

▲ ATLANTIC SPOTTED DOLPHINS, *Stenella frontalis,* Bahama Bank, page 125. I can close my eyes and still remember this day of playing with this pod of dolphins. If only I could hold my breath as long as they are able to. **Nikon F4S, Aquatica housing, Nikon 16mm lens, Fujichrome Provia 100.**

▼ ATLANTIC SPOTTED DOLPHINS, *Stenella frontalis*, Bahama Bank page 126. I enjoy photographing dolphins. They remind me that we should not take life too seriously. We all need to play once in a while. **Nikon F4S, Aquatica housing, Nikon 16mm lens, Kodak TMax 100, Ilford Multigrade paper.**

▲ ATLANTIC SPOTTED DOLPHINS, *Stenella frontalis,* Bahama Bank, page 127. These two adult spotted dolphins remind me of the saying 'older and wiser'. Spotted dolphins acquire their spots with age. **Nikon F4S, Aquatica housing, Nikon 16mm lens, Kodak TMAX 100, Ilford Multigrade paper.**

▼ MORRISON SPRING, FLORIDA, page 128. This place has always had a mystical feel for me. During the winter, a surface layer of river water moves back into the spring. This produces a halocline that gives everything a surreal look. **Nikon FE2, Ikelite housing, 17mm lens, Kodak EPP 100.**

▲ TIDAL POOL, Fernando de Noronha, Brazil, page 129. This is a 'No fins allowed' environment. Who needs them? The water is only two-to-three feet deep. This image is about light. **Nikon F4S, Aquatica housing, Nikon 18mm lens, Fujichrome Provia 100.**

▼ MOTHER AND BABY ATLANTIC SPOTTED DOLPHINS, *Stenella frontalis,* Bahama Bank, page 130. It is a very special moment when the mother dolphin allows the baby to be on the side nearest you. These two came right to me. **Nikon F4S, Aquatica housing, Nikon 16mm lens, Kodak TMAX 100 Ilford Multigrade paper.**

▲ BOTTLENOSE DOLPHIN, *Tursiops truncatus,* Gulf of Mexico, page 131. This dolphin almost looks like a piece of sculpture because of the quality of light and the dolphin's innately beautiful form. Nikon F4S, Aquatica housing, Nikon 16mm lens, Kodak TMAX 100, Ilford Multigrade paper.

▼ ATLANTIC SPOTTED DOLPHINS, *Stenella frontalis*, Bahama Bank, page 132. Nature is art, and it is up to the image-maker to see what is already there. Nikon F4S, Aquatica housing, Nikon 18mm lens, Fujichrome Provia 100.

▲ ATLANTIC SPOTTED DOLPHINS, *Stenella frontalis*, Bahama Bank, page 133. Diving with dolphins is so much fun that sometimes you forget to come up to breathe. Nikon F4S, Aquatica housing, Nikon 18mm lens, Fujichrome Provia 100.

▼ BOTTLENOSE DOLPHIN, *Tursiops truncatus,* Gulf of Mexico, page 134. I love this sort of minimalism, that seems to invite you into the image. The stark blue sky on the blue sea was a very rare day for the Gulf of Mexico. Nikon FE2, Nikon 20mm lens, Kodak EPP 100.

▲ BOTTLENOSE DOLPHINS, *Tursiops truncatus,* Gulf of Mexico, page 135. This is the same spot where the image on page 208 was taken. The circumstances are obviously a little different. These waves are the herald of the storms that come in the autumn to this area. Nikon 8008s, Nikon 28mm lens, Fujichrome Provia 100.

▼ BOTTLENOSE DOLPHINS, *Tursiops truncatus,* Gulf of Mexico, page 136. This image was made early in the morning, when there was not a puff of wind on the bay. The young dolphin cruised with us as we slowly went to sea. Nikon 8008s, Nikon 28mm lens, Fujichrome Provia 100.

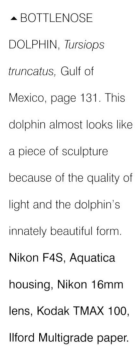

▲ BOTTLENOSE DOLPHIN, *Tursiops truncatus*, Gulf of Mexico, page 137. It is fascinating to watch a dolphin surface on a perfectly flat sea. The textures that are created seem to lead you into the image. **Nikon FE2, Nikon 20mm lens, Kodak EPP 100.**

▼ LAUGHING GULL AT DUSK, *Larus canus*, Gulf of Mexico, page 138. This was the end of a long day that was full of insights and surprises. It seems that the day had one more surprise for me. **Nikon 8008, Nikon 28mm lens, Fujichrome Provia 100.**

DONALD TIPTON

by Joe Cocozza

Donald Tipton is an eclectic and passionate soul. He lives in the moment and believes that everything will work itself out. Some would call him naive, but Don sees the world in a different light and he hears hidden notes in the blaring music. This is a man who combines his fervent belief in the divine word of scripture with his understanding of the scientific proof of natural selection, and who will explain to you at great length why these two beliefs are not incongruent.

His roots are in the southern United States. As a southern gentleman he has an all-encompassing love of his family and his God, but he defies the other associated stereotype of a southern man. He is totally without prejudice and is liberal in most (but not all) of his political beliefs. Don's first passion was, and is, classical music. He majored in music and fine arts at the University of Georgia. But in the usual way that the fates circumvent mortal plans, he did not become a concert pianist, instead becoming fascinated by the world of photography. And, as the chord structure of a Beethoven sonata can paint a picture, the tonal shading of a photograph can sing a song. Don has the ability to make music with light.

He is a firm believer in contrast. To quote Donald: 'This life we lead is a journey between the sacred and the profane'. This contrast he brings together with light and shadow. The ocean realm tends to reduce the contrast range, but this makes the subtlety of greyscale even more important – both in music and photography, it is Donald's controlled use of tone that expresses his vision and incarnates his reality.

It was 12 years ago that Donald discovered scuba diving. The sport completed his personal trinity: music, light and the sea. He immersed himself in diving and within two years was a scuba instructor and cave diver. With his passion for the sea and its creatures, underwater photography was a natural progression. Very quickly Don's star rose in the constellation of renowned underwater photographers.

Today, with the explosive growth of the sport of scuba diving and the advent of cheap underwater cameras, the standard of great underwater photography is no longer defined by technology. Talent is the determining factor in the artistic merit of an underwater photograph. What makes Don's photographs special is the range of his experience, his beliefs, and the passion that he brings to his photographic canvas.

Sometime he finds it appropriate to express his vision through boisterous and discordant colours, but many times Don takes a retro approach, expressing his vision through the soft and subdued tones of black and white photography. Using this simplicity of approach, Don expresses his unique vision of marine mammals. His images evoke moods and feelings that I struggle to describe in prose and verse. I was with Donald when he took some of these photographs and I still find it hard to describe them in words.

His images are like that awakening time, just before dawn, when some issue has been resolved in your dreams. In that brief moment before consciousness there is an understanding of the universe. It's what the Hindus call 'vidya'. The understanding is fleeting, as the mind passes into the modern world and the filters of experience diffuse understanding. Don's photos capture the twilight quality of the ocean realm.

Don's soul mate and inspiration is his wife Angelyn. She is the glue that keeps his life together. She gives his life stability. If it weren't for Angelyn, Don would subsist on a diet of Coca-Cola and Snickers bars.

I remember how, once, at an old sugar plantation in St Croix, in the West Indies, we both felt the 300-year-old karma of the slaves who had toiled and died there. We waited to photograph the 'golden hour', when the sun's low angle would produce the right shadows and glow. We sensed the cycle of life in the nearby reeds and estuaries, as creatures big and small struggled in those marshes. Don and I discussed Nietzsche and the gender of God as we clicked through roll after roll of Fujichrome.

Don and I have discussed metaphysics on the Midway Islands and survived raging storms off British Columbia. In New Orleans we have argued about Hebrew mysticism and hyperbaric physiology. While shipwreck diving off New York City we discussed the history of German U-boats. I had an epiphany with Donald as we were diving with wild dolphins and listening to Beethoven's Ninth Symphony.

Don has touched my life. Because of his art and his friendship, I have learned to see the ocean through the lens of my heart.

Thanks

Donald Tipton

Katherine Tipton

To God The Father, Son and Holy Spirit, for the creation of the sea and all the blessings that abound in life. To my wife, Angelyn, for having the patience, love and endurance to help this book happen. To my children, Jonathan, Andrew, and Katherine, for your love and smiles. To my parents, Abraham and Jean Tipton, for loving me enough to let me discover my own way. To Graeme Gourlay, for believing in me. And to Jerry Holland (for being my first diving instructor), Jim Cawthorne (for being my first photography teacher), David Doubilet (for inspiring me), Joe Cocozza, Dräger Dive, Michael Atlas, Russell McFee, Denis Richard, Robert Henno, Lee Johnson, Clay Powers, Elizabeth and everyone at Bottom Time Adventures, Kaz, Aeris Dive Gear, Ty Sawyer, Brian Courtney, Kirt Brown, Shirley Brown, Jason Belport, Tom Campbell, Alusio Campos, Patrick Mueller, Debbie Glover, John Bone, Michael Aw, The Larks, The Barnharts, Susan Anders and The Marine Mammal Center, Rabbi Tom Freedman, Dave Reed and Terry Schuler of Ultra Light, Ludwig van Beethoven and Queen Elizabeth I.